Darker Still

poems by

Ben E. Campbell

Finishing Line Press
Georgetown, Kentucky

Darker Still

ACKNOWLEDGMENTS

Thanks are due to the editors of the following publications in which some of
these poems originally appeared: *Broad River Review, The Bluestone Review,
Floyd County Moonshine,* and *Clinch Mountain Review.*

A debt of gratitude is owed as well to the West Virginia Division of Culture
and History for the bestowing of a professional development grant that
afforded respite and reflection at Moniack Mhor, the national writing centre
of Scotland.

For inspiration, guidance, and emotional support, the author wishes to
express his love and appreciation for the following individuals: Dr. John
McKernan, a creative force whose kind words and gentle nudging granted
a first-generation student the confidence to believe in his pursuits; Dr.
Richard Messer, a steadying compass in the midst of youthful storms;
those professors and workshop mates at Bowling Green State University
who assisted in setting a cornerstone; Dr. Pat Huber, President of New
River Community College, an awakener of dormant muses; Becky Ann
Campbell—beloved wife, staunch supporter, and esteemed counterbalance;
Gracie and Makinna Campbell, beacons to God's intent in a dark, relentless
world; those numerous family members and friends who have listened and
encouraged; and his working-class grandparents whose love and leading
lessons brought focus to a life.

Publisher: Leah Huete de Maines
Editor: Christen Kincaid
Cover Art: *Tipple Ruins,* by Cris Ritchie of Hazard, Kentucky
Author Photo: *Miners' Memorial, Quinwood, WV,* by Becky Campbell
Cover Design: Elizabeth Maines McCleavy

Order online: www.finishinglinepress.com
also available on amazon.com

Author inquiries and mail orders:
Finishing Line Press
P. O. Box 1626
Georgetown, Kentucky 40324
U. S. A.

Table of Contents

I. Lament

Return 1

Black-Lung Miner Eulogy 2

Miner's Tale in Three Acts 3

Soup Bean Supper 4

Panoramic Picture 5

The Lonely Hour 6

Persimmon Seed Sign 7

II. Teach

Ramp Patch 8

Hewer's Feast 10

Beneath 11

Foot Washing 12

Stacking Wood 13

Crushing 14

III. Honor

Sleepwalk 17

Winter's Beard 18

Canning 19

1960s Coal-Camp House Code 20

Memory 21

IV. Speak

Echo 23

His Unknown Prayer 24

His Known Prayer 25

Thank-You Note to Her 26

Miner's Math 27

The Coal Miner's Grandson 28

Penance 29

Darker Still 31

*Dedicated to the memory of
my Appalachian Opa,
Jack D. Hoover*

I. Lament

Return

I walked your house's floors
last night through lens of dusky dream,
alone in still-struck basement,
the tokens of your hand work
massed beneath the structure's groin:
the coal bin filled to chute mouth,
stacked row of rusted cans
where you ushered nuts and bolts.
I thought I heard you there
in the echoes of my steps,
walking back through mothball scent
clinging nooks and darkened corners.
Alas, it was not you though
but a draft of stolen air,
wind sucked through tarp-patched window,
a nagging, forlorn sigh.

I. Lament

Black-Lung Miner Eulogy

He knew of carnal darkness
before darkness knew of him,
before the sprout of coal-charred roots
broke free from dampened floors—
before time even—
a black so dark he could taste
its belched-up soot,
feel crawl beneath the
surface of his deepest, pulsing vein.
The Earth he disemboweled with
a butcher's common grace,
and by anthracrosis' touch
he'll grow hollow just the same.
Ashes to dust and dust corroding vapor,
to the ground this dredger crawls.
Let no one carve on rivaled stone
by granite hastened words.
For a diamond trails not coal
when forged from earthly pressure,
nor a river flooding time
beyond a mountain's unveiled tear.

I. Lament

Miner's Tale in Three Acts

I.

Morning met by mountain shadow loom, daylight breaks the tree-scalped crest through a frosted window prism, dawn rise now at fourteen years like all he's ever known, whispered words to make it real through a pass of standing breath: "Lord, but it is cold!" Learning's for the learned he once learned, so no rush to school house made. It'll do to run the ridgelines, sloshing bottles, burlap bags, or in hollows' winding traipse scoping bead on branded deer, hauling something more than words to the evening's supper table. Child, until dark mines makes room for one more man, the cold of morning nulled in his trek beneath the ground, climate steady and even tempered. Settle fully into scene.

II.

Days burned by ray of candled crown, he traverses same drawn path beneath the mountain's bulging bottom: light in darkness, light in darkness, light in darkness; no sun to pierce the darkness. At home a thriving brood, five bodies milled by mold. Hungry mouths make holes in hungry hearts, bending men to furtive worry. Only work can fill the void where meat supplants the bread. Work of day, work of night. Work of never-ending week. Work to bury thought of work. In sparse and spacious hour where no darkness drags, descends, he ticks glass with dusty nail, keeping time through hollowed light in brown, reflective bottle. Fade to forty years this way passed.

III.

Stone-on-stone abrasion rubs bone like strike of flint, whole of insides set to flame amid the smolder of two crushings. Dig he cannot stop, forged grit his lasting shovel, small comfort bounty aim. Nights mesh thrash to an endless coughing chorus, spraying black the red-dot kerchief long last waved at base of Blair. It'll do to catch his breath, to pass the press of cringing hour without slab upon drawn chest. He drills through crawl of yesteryear flashing moments, captured sights: the touch of child's small hand, mangled leg of fellow miner pinched by track-jumped car. His greatest dug-up treasure in the wisdom of learned woes—one cannot prop with rotted pillars. Lights go out like shuttered mines. No bow at curtain's call.

I. Lament

Soup Bean Supper

One cannot fill a poor
man's bowl by the
harvest of coke and cinder.
Want to feed a ravaged body?
Ladle soup beans over
corn bread so he may
dredge a crumbled mound,
auger hunger just as Grandpa did
by heft of force-bent spoon.
Our last supper I recall
he gorged on mess'a beans,
sharing praise for lifelong bounty
through chomp and singsong slurp.
Father who art in Heaven,
he gave thanks for seasoned kettle,
for souls called gathered 'round,
for light that coal mines fueled
that he may read a diner's work.
Let sustenance rain like
manna on yon hill,
over haunting conjured face,
stored rasp of hard-drawn breath.
No vessel fills his table end.
Only grit of grainy bean,
the breaking time-staled bread.
These customs proxy remnants
feeding hunger left by void.

I. Lament

Panoramic Picture

"That man's on both sides," the young boy yawps.
The same gaunt man propping up the photo's ends
like a slouched and crooked pillar.
Must be voodoo picture magic.
Black-and-white voodoo by way of West-by-God.
But of all them dirtied-up men posing
still beyond the hole,
how's come he should get both ends?
What makes him a better miner than
the feller centered left, the short and indiscreet one,
proud man whose room photo adorns
over stack of handstitched quilts?
Why not him as company bookends?
Touch here the dip in bed where he
passes nightly worry,
the threat of suffocation like a hill above his head.
Hear the take of ticking clock
on the metage of lost life,
thirty-six years as stand-in statue.
Breathe scent of dime-store ointment
as it floats like soot on air.
And look, look long upon dark room,
this plain and simple room—an incomplete picture
of the man who made it whole—and tell me
straight-faced fully: why not him
to get the honor he so outwardly deserves?

I. Lament

The Lonely Hour

Three cars ahead
they charge through faulted fence:
two does in primal flight,
shared hunt for higher ground.
I watch from my closed space
time slow to palsied still,
myself and no one else
to mark graceless fates collide,
both clipped in one swift flash
skidding flailed beyond bruised hood.
In this daily hour drive
where seclusion leads to lull,
and I drag my thought of you
on bed of drawn-out death,
a gush of heightened sense
stirs life to inert blood.
Driving past the instant carnage,
first one spared a prolonged pain,
I catch the sheen-glossed eye
of the second kicking air,
bulged pupil rounding search
for small sign of longed companion.
"Be still," I speak aloud
in the cramped, constraining void.
"You are destined for that field
where you'll never roam alone."

I. Lament

Persimmon Seed Sign

These barren hills speak of you.
They are weathered, beaten, worn,
reversed to infant state
by their naked, ordered change.
What I would do to restore them,
to mend to summer's peak
buoyant life through lush of tree—
make green what loss has browned.

You looked frail at dusk of death,
unlike the man I knew
who had shouldered mountain load.
I would have given my own April
to help you breathe, to move black
from tarnished lung, to make all that
you then suffered but a bout of locust frost.

First changeover since your parting
I sliced persimmon seed in palm,
searching halves for folktale sign,
that gauge of trusted forecast
by the seers of your day:
fork-shape revealed makes
for brush of breezy season,
knife conclusive sign of a
sharp and dragging wind.

It grows cold here now,
the threat of winter looming,
a long, for-darkened era
that may never cease to cut.

II. Teach

Ramp Patch

"Come," he calls again.
"Come stand. Come watch. Come listen."
"Come" that unceasing, drawled command,
familiar prelude to a lecture.
But come from up above
makes for come that's meant to move,
spur one off his idle haunches.

"Come" wade through maze of stone,
beyond tangled rhododendron,
up hillside drowned in brown
bearing early season's print,
lone green the sprouted shoots
of ramps from rising graves.

"Come" to swing at rebuilt hip
shovel's finger-ticking sway,
dulled end dusted black from
wayward lumps of coal,
black jewels that I corralled
during other beckoned come.

Come I do in doubled time,
thrusting shovel as I'm shown,
rich blood of loosened soil
spilled in clumps about boot feet,
plunge mindful of the bulb
to spare life where life can render.

II. Teach

In span of nonstop hour
we two strip the mountain clean,
filling pails of paper pokes
past bloated, bulging point,
the odor of ramp capture
wafting restless on stirred wind.

At truck he breaks from word,
making known through heavy nod
his content with what was taken,
"come" at calm for long drive home
through the shucked and silent hills—
until kitchen table's spread calls
for hands to come once more.

Resting bounty on the bed,
I pull stalk to light of day,
its leafy end wilted
from the mangle of the haul,
and clinch in tightened palm
sacred offering of our dig.
"Come" crushed to fossil print.

II. Teach

Hewer's Feast

Entrapped in cast-iron haze of culled and toppled taters,
by kitchen-counter lean I thumb the dinted pail,
dull metal peeking out amid a cloak of time-worn seals:
U.M.W.A., Copenhagen, second home to lifelong work—
long tipple up the hill meeting slant of ridgeline crest,
deep mines set in place to feed a nation's voltage hunger.
The clang of doled-out plates rattles space beyond the wall
as I trace the crooked row, resting thumb at OSHA label.
Black-diamond warrior I'm to be, I tug its loosened end,
painting face on future bucket through a smudge of dusty dream,
its innards altered layers: Little Debbies, Sunday ham.
Across the drawn-in room he must make my seam of thought,
spading rocks of years-long recall for a moment's cornered morsel.
He stands at "y'all come on" to usher us to table,
shedding perch on barstool edge to rip the emblem clean.
"Careful what you touch," he says, then hacks a hardened cough.
"Some things don't come off. Now go wash yourself for supper."

II. Teach

Beneath

There was that time once
when in couch's comfort grip
I was moved by call below,
skipping basement's staggered stairs
two warped boards with each harsh leap.
Burrowed, as you in lowly mines,
I could feel the coal stove flushed
from the bloat of force-fed meal,
and through whiff of lazy belches
make the smells of work beneath:
buttered apples, self-canned beans, cellared yams—
nothing given, your keen mantra, only earned.
"Here," you barked behind the part of worn bedsheet
wall, you straddling strung-up deer,
pulling hide from lifeless carcass,
slow drip of steady blood flecking
floors of pristine keep.
"Them," you said with nod to nearby stool,
sheathed knife and dulling saw
set in wait to do your bidding.
I did my passing part then watched by
backward trek you hack to heightened fury,
cutting hams from hinds and shoulders,
no protest from doe eyes
gone glossed with passive death.
The loin that you called tender you
held firmly to my face,
flicking spray of rationed blood
against my taut and endless flinch.
"Take it to your grandma," you instructed.
"And hurry, lest it spoil and be no good."

II. Teach

Foot Washing

No trace of barren flesh
spared mark by dark trade's hand—
miner's daily bath staking
claim to every fold—
I knew only dust-lined brows,
of fingers streaking charcoal
by brush of blackened nail.
The sacred he revealed in
Sunday service midst,
stripping shoe and woolen sock
to the core of bone-white foot,
that space beyond the touched
where a guarded fraction dwelled.
Faithful servant to that house,
he took other's foot to hand
above river's plastic basin,
running palms callused coarse
through waters crystal clear,
stirring softly before wash
that elixir blessed to cleanse.
The year's gathered sin
he rinsed gentle by his stroke,
no tense or rapid motion
as was custom to his touch,
no protest as like Peter
when by Christ he was entrusted.
In the act of joint exchange
he sat solemn in his stance,
released from mountain bondage:
stilled calm to stormy hands,
soothed tapping pound at foot.
Enraptured in my pew
cushioned bleeding velvet red,
I found by his divide
that sweet wine that
makes one whole,
a living water's stream.

Stacking Wood

Break from winter's snare,
I tour the mussed-up stack,
this audit set to motion like a
theft of Frost's famed poem.
Only stone here cuts no ground.
Heaped wood has birthed this wall,
eight ricks grown slouching graceless
from the winds of frost-drawn breath.
"Stack to season," my grandfather urges
through lesson seared in time,
his edict like an echo
riding tail of rustled breeze.
Bending, I gather wayward log to
the cradle of my bosom,
inspecting ring-laced bottom
weathered dull since Fall's mauled split.
Time caught in clinging years,
I am forced to lift the thought:
what will mark this simple task
come the row of future days?
The make of cold-brow sweat
amid this grey and vapid hollow?
The memory of that coaching
long lost to work-bred hands?
Or the knowledge that what calls here
will burn hot to holy ash?

II. Teach

Crushing

And the dreaded phone call came,
no omen to precede it
as is known to be the case.
No star streaked dropping from the sky.
No bird smacked dead against a window.
Just the news that you'd been crushed.
Common learnings in our parts.
Kinfolk always prepare. They just fail to be prepared.

I was outside mowing grass,
earning keep as you had learned me,
breathing air of early June.
She there met me on a turn swipe,
urging headphones off my ears.
"There's been an accident," she said.
"Your PaPaw's been crushed."

Mad dash for Morgantown later,
shucking curves in rusted car,
we spilled into that small room,
you so flat on sick-man's bed
like a slab upon our chests,
my own lungs seemingly crippled.
Pain like the writhing that you wore
could cause a man to curse the mines,
the backbone of our state.
Heretics are often born in such ways.

"It's his hip," MaMaw told us,
torn but keeping it in,
playing role of miner's wife.
"His hip's been crushed."
How many fits of broken bone
does it take for us to learn?
This your second in thirty-six years.
Most men drop dead at their first crushing,
but you were too stubborn, too charged.

II. Teach

I thought that I might cry.
The room felt closed in on me.
I didn't know it at the time,
but they call me claustrophobic,
for my fear of tightened space.
It was tight in that room,
with kin and working machines.

Your eldest didn't help matters,
ranting as she did,
and not about you, or the mines,
or even West Virginia,
which was starting to feel like a
rat trap set by God.
Just the same ol', same ol'.
Her husband didn't come.
He doesn't love her.
No one gets her mortal pain.

"Have a look!" I wanted to shout,
and point at your long cringe.
"That is truly pain!"
But no one said a word.
They were all used to it by then,
to everything—from phone calls
to Bi-Polar soliloquies.

This is our world.
This is our world?

You called my name twice.
I stepped closer second time,
to bedside's cramped-up space,
tucking my lanky arms.
I even grabbed your hand,
which you then squeezed
a long, hard minute,
hot pain in radiation.

II. Teach

What will I do when my own
crushing comes? I thought.
Who will crowd by my hospital bed?
Whose name will I call twice?

"It'll be all right," I thought I heard.
"*I* will be all right," I wanted to hear, from you,
from a semblance of yourself.
I could have stood for,
"Don't go into the mines."
Or, "I'd be proud of you just the same."

Instead, "It's the medicine," someone
offered at the sight of my drawn face,
landing hope a crushing blow.

That's the thing your crushing learned me then,
what I took about this place.
Rock don't have to crumble,
nor machine to run a rail.
We've got all we'll ever need
in the pillars of our bones
to meet call of our sewn fate,
lives pressed like fossils into hills,
those dark, foreboding spaces
where we shun the path to light.

III. Honor

Sleepwalk

Somewhere in that vacuum
between racing up blue dawn

and blessing back before the door
she made peace with rising day,

day sifting after day,
blurred haze from window street lamp

by the step of darkened know
like a dreamscape plunging fall.

Gagged birds about the nest,
low moon in sulking brood,

she moved soundless over time
as if caught in fit of sleepwalk,

fitting pail with measured bread,
gracing handle whispered prayer

from what woke—a safe return—
eyes clinched 'til day has closed.

So much that goes unsaid
in the archives of lost sleep,

a story she once penned
brailleing hands by heart's devotion,

sculpting shrine through unseen stone
amidst dearth of longed-for light.

III. Honor

Winter Beard

Cold so sharp it could
cut through age-packed coal, into
thumb-choked grip of
season's ceaseless strangle.
But below the crusted ground
he makes haste by heated work,
sweat beads dripping blackened brow
in rage of worker's thaw.
Praise be their filthy gutter,
winter beard of deer-death growth.
For when he crawls from dampened murk
it will buffer loathsome blow,
slow sting of solstice snare
as it does for wife's drawn biding,
the sink-rim trimmings
that she dabs
like sparks of muted flame,
loose embers holding heat
before warmth is welcomed home.

III. Honor

Canning

Harvest procured from droopy belly vines—
table-topped tomatoes flaring red, tense

beans succumbed to snapping—she tracks
slant of midday sun to a basking, upturned jar,

its name print bearing dirt smudge in bulged
and curving crevice. So many years, she thinks,

a party to this practice, this act of preservation
she could captain through lost sleep.

Wiping what immersion failed to wash,
she turns back to stovetop kettle, steering fleet

of bobbing glass about the boiling water's sea.
Beyond the rising hills out sliver-window view

her husband feasts on flora churned to
centuries-hoarded methane, crawling seams as

cramped as shelves lining hidden basement walls.
Adrift, she chokes grip on fraying dish towel

at the pop of first-sealed jar, signaling what
she does not know by the gathered silence cracked.

III. Honor

1960s Coal-Camp House Code

Cleanliness is Next to Godliness

> These words inscribed in wood
> make for mantra above door,
> holy waters to veiled dirt
> floating house as dusty spirits.

A Penny Pinched is a Hunger Cinched

> Meat on Sunday solely,
> she culls menu out of air,
> stretching garden's bounty goods
> to the peak of frugal heights.

The Back was Built for Bending

> If he can stoop I
> can stoop if he can
> bend I can bend
> our work we merrily blend!

You Could Eat from Off Those Floors

> Issued decree in coal-camp store aisle,
> she wears knees a royal purple
> scrubbing floors of beveled groove,
> guarded quest to hold lone crown.

Blue Jays Crowd the Bird Box

> The view from kitchen sink
> confirms the law of land:
> the brightest of this world
> take all for their own pleasure.

III. Honor

Memory

Too little shared too late,
fate would have its languished say
in the constructs of her mind,
spewing fog through memory's labyrinth
as it willed its slow submission.
She did not know me on that day,
thinking me her younger brother,
a sideways grasp at kinship
when as grandson I was down.
I dared not offer up correction,
not when compass of sure thought
pulled her back to precious place,
lone setting stuck on repeat:
that tree at yard's cleared edge
in the home place of "our" youth,
its tips in white-washed blossom,
vast hollow sprouted green.
Atop mother's fabled quilt
bleeding thin its faded color
we place hands to upward reach,
dotted sun in grasp above,
spread lunch about our feet
in a mass to feed a lifetime.

But then the unseen switch,
the one that holds us hostage
to sought worlds we cannot own.
"I knew," she went astray,
staring through the window's glare,
past autumn's stripped-down oaks
on distant mountain's peak.
"I knew all those men, and
when I saw them on the porch…"
the cliff that she there built

III. Honor

above the bloom of dangled thought
rearing steep and endless drop.
They had come there bearing news,
making new news from time's ash,
fresh worry welling up in her
dark and moistened eyes.

I did not need to know the rest—
that tale of family lore.
The mines had crushed her soul half,
had split his bone from flesh
as a meaning ripped from moment.
I could only let her linger
for the briefest drawn-out breath,
such pain a pointless torture.

"Do you remember?" I calmly posed,
"That picnic at the home place?"
Our circle rounded corner
by the break of blushing smile.
More a Mobius strip I thought
in urge to scourge us clean,
remiss to memory's impulse
for clearing bent and aimless paths,
the fruit of what we've mustered
still to wrestle from the branch.

IV. Speak

Echo

Words were like
burbling pools of water
skinning river barren stone,
soft touch allotted light
where the darkened cove transcends,
starving trout to heightened blindness.

I could sense but could not seize
hot flash of nascent thought,
my tongue a tied-up tangle—
taut braid, Suebiac knot—
speech squeezed to guttural grunt.
But I was here I was here.

I stood at mountain's edge
where star meets blossomed cloud
and watched through frame unfold
swift lapse, the binding breath
leading dark to day make merge
time's call to pious union

And in sensory-drunken gorge
of sight and sound and touch
I loosened sonant yawp
that in flight divinely fell,
remnant resting tremored leaf—

                              hanging,
like last note of Nero's fiddle.

IV. Speak

His Unknown Prayer

God, curse the shovel's end—
not the pick, the hammer, the wedge:
    They feed hunger, furnish need.

God, dig this pain a grave—
I did not share its haunting hurt:
    I had charge to head a household.

God, turn the hands of time—
breathe life to powdered dust:
    I saw death not fashioned in fossil face.

God, soothe my blistered hands—
I can't stab this stubborn ground:
    Turn handle of oak to molten ash.

God, burn a sacred bush—
send balm that aims to heal:
    These sights I can't carve from blemished eye.

God, wilt the shovel's end—
I dug graves for my own blood:
    Not all holes make certain miner's glory.

IV. Speak

His Known Prayer

Graceful be the day break by frosted autumn dawn,
    first breath beyond the house
        reaching back to newborn gasp.

Praise the stock truck's trout,
    may they starve an angler's hunger
        in their thrash against cast line.

Glory to the deer stand in its highest crowning steeple,
    or by swollen tree trunk's flank
        hunter's blend to bleed the wild.

Blessed are the woods sprouting oak, maple, ash,
    tall poplar stretching upward for a
        brush from Heaven hand.

Hail the darkened mines and its ever-winding
    seams, procurer of the paycheck
        feeding starving body's flesh.

Thanks to time's long voyage, for the path
    of gathered days. Amen appreciation,
        amen my honest word.

IV. Speak

Thank-You Note to Her

What would I have said had I known my way by word, if I had curbed
my tongue at hand, if the scroll of pen to paper had then bloomed at
finger's tip? I did not learn to read or write in the apex of my time, and
not by will of sheer defiance. I had a world to wage a war with, those
Randolph County hills so bent on bleeding youth, on molding mind
and hand to a pick-axe, saw, or shovel. The need to furnish food starved
out pangs of learner's hunger. So you became my eyes. You became my
ears. You became my voice. On you I leaned my senses. I could not
have crawled this world otherwise. Even by speech I felt beholden. I
did not know the words to say, how to carve my racing thoughts. I only
wish that I'd said more, that the seam of my true thanks had been bared
for your heart's mining. My touch is lost to time, no blessing for your
grace etched in seal of lavish parchment. Let this poem stand as mark
that you spoke two to being one.

IV. Speak

Miner's Math

You never met your father's dad,
the seed of your translucence.
He made a specter of his name
in the year your father bloomed.
Five kids and a carry-all wife
and still he tramped away,
into the arms of wanton love.
And you, you never glimpsed his
turn-coat eyes, never pored
those chronicled annals.
What does it mean to leap
a number, to pass
claim of derivation
from a man who died alone?
You too would sire five kids,
carved-out emblems of your total.
But manhood made by math
rarely lands at one true sum.
Like the feat of yonder years
measured up by gathered ton:
the scales were always rigged
to usher favor for the system.
Yet still you persevered, beating
odds no baron dare bet,
and all without long roots to
lead you back to one true home.
How keen the calculation
when you left a buried past
undefined by slag-like bones.

IV. Speak

The Coal Miner's Grandson

What he was
was not like you—
a feral river's stream,
dulled point of mountain's arch.
Where pick met brawn
in the crease of callused hand,
you could only proffer palms
turned soft as binded paper.
Yet still you mined coarse veins,
resolved to matching blood
cutting crease to common core.
What you must have seemed to him
through dank and dusty eye,
first born to his own first born,
brash shirker of the dirt.
Throw off the narrowed spaces
he crawled closer through to God,
but hunker where you stand.
He is swallowed now,
his parting like a light
gone lost within the shaft.
You calling into darkness,
here lost on hollow ground.

IV. Speak

Penance

I am me
not of then
not of who
I nulled creation
I am rebirth
brought to pass
I am someone
some the same.

In print of
paling line
I transgressed against
our claim
to hand
to blood
to dirt
shunning plunge of
calloused palm
into entrails
dressing deer,
your gift in
hardened love that
I may feed
a fading instinct
that I may stitch
a failing nerve.

As penance
I will bear
what shame
can here to cleanse—
I will wash
my face in sun
I will sing
the song of leaves
I will offer
through mined words

IV. Speak

by psalm
a binding branch
to grasp,
by blood beneath
clean nails
a home to
yearned and
owned forgiveness.

IV. Speak

Darker Still

The world this long day
without you in casting light
turned shades darker still

Ben E. Campbell was born in 1976, in the Allegheny Highlands of Greenbrier County, West Virginia. He graduated from Marshall University with degrees in Psychology and Adult and Continuing Education, and earned the M.F.A. in fiction writing from Bowling Green State University, where he was the recipient of a Devine fellowship. His writings have appeared in more than three dozen literary venues to date, including *New Plains Review, Roanoke Review, Now and Then,* and *Yemassee.* In 2016 he was awarded a professional development grant from the West Virginia Division of Culture and History for his creative and scholarly efforts. His writing has also received awards from the Appalachian Heritage Writers Symposium, West Virginia Writers, Inc. and the LMU Mountain Heritage Literary Festival. He is the author of the short story collection *A Welcome Walk into the Dark.* Ben resides in Lewisburg, West Virginia with his wife and two daughters.

CPSIA information can be obtained
at www.ICGtesting.com
Printed in the USA
BVHW030055171120
593326BV00002B/136